To my family, and especially to Zerg: Thanks for being the best road-trip buddy on this great journey I could ever ask for. —K.L.

For Dominic—keep your wheels turning and your engine humming! —M.S.

MAGIC CAT PUBLISHING

The 50 States Things That Go © 2025 Lucky Cat Publishing Ltd
Text by Kristen Lee
Illustrations © 2025 Martin Stanev
First Published in 2025 by Magic Cat Publishing, an imprint of Lucky Cat Publishing Ltd,
Unit 2 Empress Works, 24 Grove Passage, London E2 9FQ, UK
EU Authorised Representative Magic Cat Publishing, an imprint of Lucky Cat Publishing Ltd,
PAKTA svetovanje d.o.o., Stegne 33, Ljubljana, Slovenia

The right of Martin Stanev to be identified as the illustrator of this work has been asserted by them in accordance with the Copyright, Designs and Patents Act, 1988 (UK).

No part of this publication may be reproduced, stored in a retrieval system, or transmitted, in any form, or by any means, electrical, mechanical, photocopying, recording or otherwise without the prior written permission of the publisher or a licence permitting restricted copying.

A catalogue record for this book is available from the British Library.

ISBN 978-1-915569-82-0

The illustrations were created digitally
Set in Noto Sans and Noyh

Published by Rachel Williams and Jenny Broom
Designed by Nicola Price and Clarisse Hassan
Edited by Helen Brown and Mary Jones

Manufactured in China

9 8 7 6 5 4 3 2 1

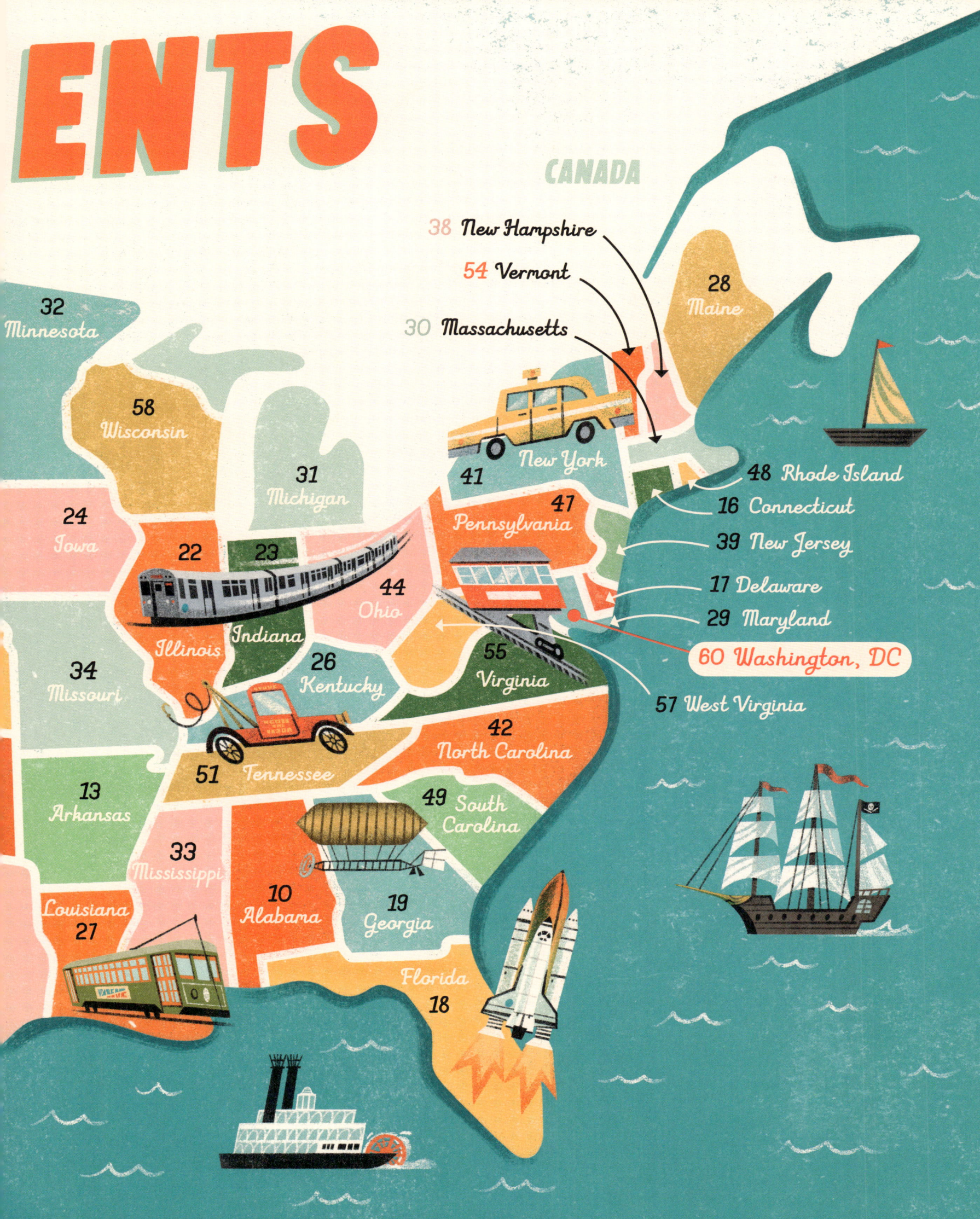

Transportation is part of America's history, from boats and rafts crafted by Indigenous peoples to the Wright brothers' first flight to the space program. Americans have come up with a lot of different ways to get going over the years, that's for sure!

There are more than 330 million people living in the United States, and all of them need to get around somehow. There are **TRAINS** and **PLANES**, **TRUCKS** and **CARS**, and the **TRAIN STATIONS**, **AIRPORTS**, and **HIGHWAYS** that support them.

This book explores how we move through all 50 of our wonderful states. And we also take a look at our capital—Washington, DC. There's a lot of land to cover, and sometimes walking just isn't enough. So let's get moving. Turn the page and see how things **GO**!

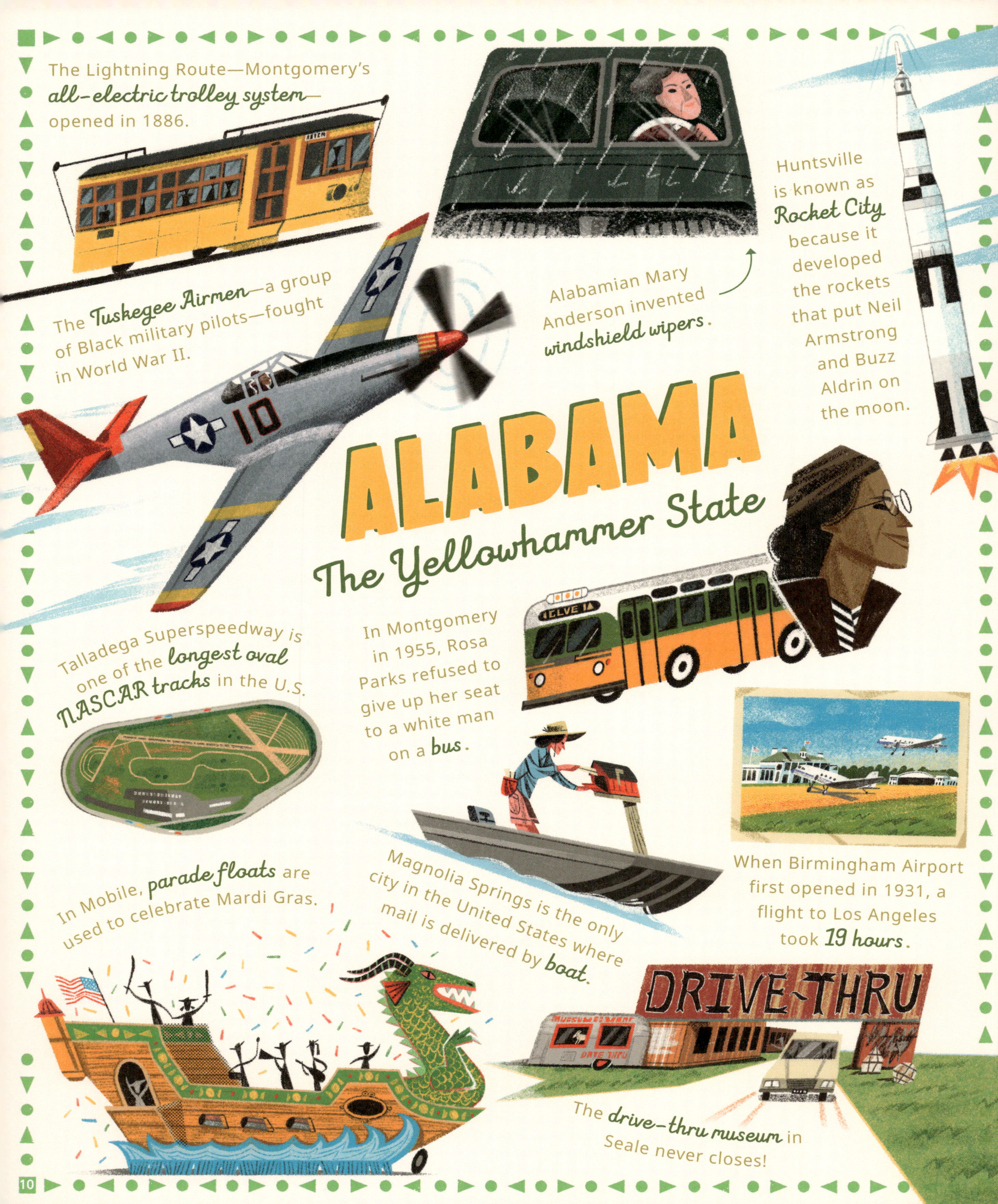

Pima Air and Space Museum displays nearly 400 aircrafts.

In 2016, *daredevil pilots* took part in a wing suit racing competition over Arizona desert.

In 2021, a man took a *tule reed raft*—like those once used by the Cocopah and Mojave—through the Grand Canyon.

Arizona has nearly 40,000 miles of *off-road trails*.

The first-ever McDonald's *drive-thru* was in Arizona.

Over half a million people have taken *Grand Canyon mule rides* since 1887.

Fishing and *boating* on Lake Havasu brings in 750,000 visitors a year.

England's original *London Bridge* was shipped and rebuilt in Lake Havasu City.

ARIZONA
The Grand Canyon State

The *Grand Canyon Train* runs on recycled vegetable oil from fast-food restaurants.

Arizona *National Guard helicopters* use Bambi Buckets to drop water on wildfires.

ARKANSAS
The Natural State

Diamond diggers operate at Murfreesboro's Crater of Diamonds State Park.

The state once had ostrich-pulled wagons.

The first steamboat to sail up the Arkansas River was called The Comet.

The historic Metro Streetcar runs through Little Rock.

US president and Arkansas native Bill Clinton owned an El Camino.

At 108 miles, the Ouachita National Recreation Trail is the longest mountain bike trail in the state.

The Caddo River has a 1.5-mile tube route!

It's illegal to honk your car horn at a sandwich shop after 9 p.m. in Little Rock.

There's an annual garden tiller race in Emerson.

The Bobby Hopper Tunnel is the only highway tunnel in Arkansas.

A *shipwreck* dating back to the American Revolution was discovered in the waters near Lewes.

The *Delaware Double Cross* is a 61-mile bike race in which participants cross the small state—twice!

Wilmington is North America's number one port for deliveries of *bananas*!

Musician Bob Marley once had a job building *cars* in Newark.

The *Cape May-Lewes Ferry* has sailed across the Delaware Bay more than 80,000 times.

The *fire engine ride* at Rehoboth Beach's Funland has been operating since it began over 60 summers ago.

The Apollo program *space suits* were invented in Delaware.

Off the coast of Slaughter Beach, Redbird Reef is made of retired New York City *subway cars*.

DELAWARE
The First State

There were once *pirates* in Delaware Bay.

A classic *black-and-white* Delaware license plate sold for $410,000 at auction.

17

Atlanta's *Hartsfield-Jackson Airport* is the busiest in the world.

At just 33 feet long, the *Stovall Mill Covered Bridge* is the smallest covered bridge in Georgia.

The *Strobel Airship*, one of the earliest dirigible balloons, flew over Savannah in 1909.

Held in Braselton, the *Petit Le Mans* is an endurance race that lasts for 1,000 miles or 10 hours—whichever comes first.

Downtown Atlanta boasts the world's largest *drive-in restaurant*.

The 1819 Savannah was the first *ship with steam power* to cross the Atlantic Ocean.

Tybee Island Lighthouse is the tallest and oldest lighthouse in Georgia.

Georgia-born *C. W. Chappelle* invented a long-distance airplane in 1911.

In Morganton's Tank Town USA, visitors can *drive a tank* over junk cars.

A *dragon boat* race is held annually on Lake Lanier.

GEORGIA
The Peach State

Idaho has more *whitewater river miles* than any other state.

The *Sacajawea Historic Byway* runs through the state for 135 miles.

The *Guffey Railroad Bridge* was once used to transport gold and silver ore.

Mule deer use the state's *wildlife overpass* to cross the highway safely.

The St. Joe River is the *highest navigable river* in the world.

IDAHO
The Gem State

Daredevil Evel Knievel tried to jump Snake River using a *steam-powered rocket*.

Early NASA astronauts visited the *Craters of the Moon National Monument* to train for space travel.

The *Silverwood Theme Park* is the biggest theme and water park in the northwest.

Idaho has the *longest gondola ride* in North America—a 3.1-mile journey.

The world's first *ski lift* was installed in Sun Valley.

ILLINOIS
The Prairie State

A plane takes off or lands at the Chicago's O'Hare International Airport every 23 seconds.

A Boeing 727 was dropped in the lake at the Mermet Springs diving site after being used to shoot a film.

The Volo Museum is home to a roller skate car. It's fully drivable and 14 feet high!

Union's Illinois Railway Museum is the largest railroad museum in the United States.

The world's first Ferris wheel was displayed at the Chicago World's Fair in 1893.

A mechanic in Clinton built a drivable upside-down truck.

Chicago is known as America's railroad capital.

Chicago is famous for the elevated "L" trains in its downtown area.

The first roller derby was held in Chicago.

An iconic fleet of yellow water taxis run across the Chicago River.

INDIANA
The Hoosier State

Twelve Mile hosts an annual **lawnmower race** on Independence Day.

The largest children's museum is in Indiana—and has an **indoor carousel**.

The **Slippery Noodle Inn** in Indianapolis was a stop on the Underground Railroad. Enslaved people would stay in the building's basement while on their journeys to freedom.

Gondolas drift serenely in White River State Park.

North Judson's **Hoosier Valley Railroad Museum** offers a ride in a vintage diesel locomotive.

Studebaker automobiles were made in South Bend.

Elkhart is known as the "**RV capital of the world.**"

The state is home to the first racing circuit to be called a "**speedway.**"

The first **gas pump** was invented in Fort Wayne in 1885.

Evansville's LST-325 is one of only two **World War II landing ship tanks (LSTs)** in America.

23

KANSAS
The Sunflower State

The Salt Mine Express in Hutchinson takes you 650 feet below ground.

Combines harvest wheat—the state's largest crop.

There's a replica of Dorothy's home in **The Wizard of Oz** in Liberal.

West Mineral's **Big Brutus** is the world's largest electric shovel.

Amelia Earhart, the first woman to fly solo across the Atlantic Ocean, was born in Atchison.

Brush Creek is a historic bridge along Route 66.

Kansans William Purvis and Charles Wilson received the first US patent for a **helicopter** in 1910.

Storm chaser vehicles are used in "Tornado Alley" states like Kansas.

Kansas's first *locomotive* ran on tracks laid at Elwood.

A Topeka museum honors *motorcycle jumper* Evel Knievel.

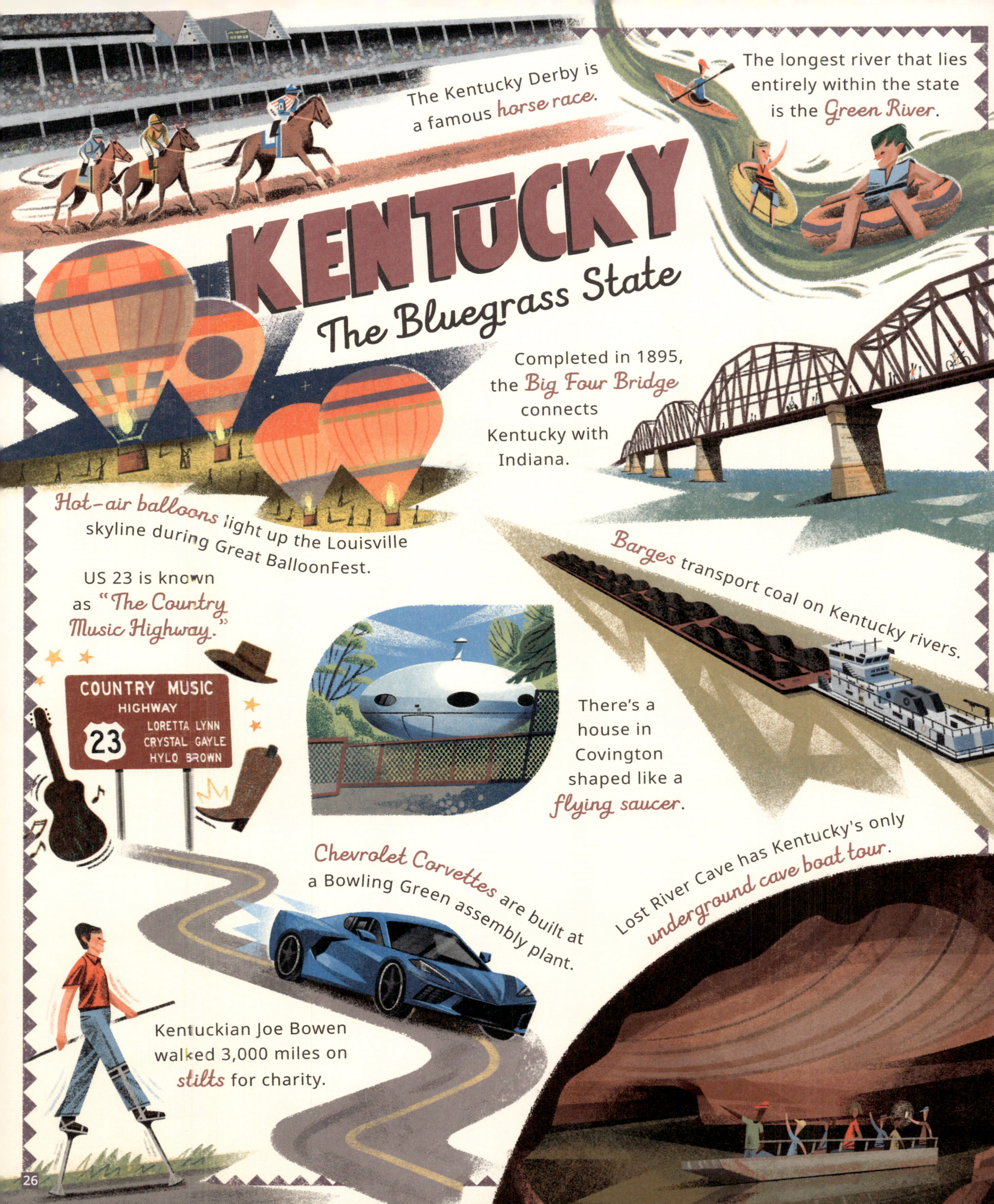

KENTUCKY
The Bluegrass State

The Kentucky Derby is a famous *horse race*.

The longest river that lies entirely within the state is the *Green River*.

Completed in 1895, the *Big Four Bridge* connects Kentucky with Indiana.

Hot-air balloons light up the Louisville skyline during Great BalloonFest.

Barges transport coal on Kentucky rivers.

US 23 is known as "*The Country Music Highway*."

There's a house in Covington shaped like a *flying saucer*.

Chevrolet Corvettes are built at a Bowling Green assembly plant.

Lost River Cave has Kentucky's only *underground cave boat tour*.

Kentuckian Joe Bowen walked 3,000 miles on *stilts* for charity.

The 24-mile **Lake Pontchartrain Causeway** is the world's longest bridge over water.

Held in DeQuincy, the **Louisiana Railroad Days Festival** features a model train show.

The **Ponchatoula Strawberry Festival Parade** celebrates the town's harvest.

NASA's Michaud Assembly Facility in New Orleans is known as "**America's Rocket Factory.**"

During **Mardi Gras**, floats parade the streets of New Orleans.

The world's **largest heliport** is in Morgan City.

When it opened in 1884, the **Crescent City Roller Skating Rink** was the largest in the country.

The Louisiana-built **American Queen** is said to be the largest river steamboat ever built.

The St. **Charles Avenue Line** is one of the world's oldest continuously operating streetcar systems.

The slow-moving **Bayou Teche** is perfect for **kayaking**.

LOUISIANA
The Pelican State

MAINE
The Pine Tree State

Specialized **lobster boats** catch the majority of the US lobster haul.

Maine is home of the U.S. National **Toboggan** Championship!

The National UFO Reporting Center reports dozens of **UFO sightings** in Maine each year.

Fort Kent marks the beginning of US Route 1, known as **America's First Mile**.

Riders stuff raw eggs in their snowmobile snowsuits before the annual **Pine Tree Camp Egg Ride** in Hermon.

Maine has more miles of **whitewater rafting** than the rest of New England and New York combined

Fifty-one miles of **carriage trails** in Acadia National Park were donated by John D. Rockefeller Jr.

Excalibur is the only wooden roller coaster in Maine.

Visitors to the "haunted" **Wood Island lighthouse** have reported seeing ghosts roam.

The **Penobscot Narrows Bridge** is Maine's longest bridge and has the highest bridge observatory in the world.

MASSACHUSETTS
The Bay State

One of the first *gas powered fire engines* was built in Springfield in 1905.

In 2018, engineers at the Massachusetts Institute of Technology designed an airplane that flies *without fuel*.

Brothers Frank and Charles Duryea made history in Springfield with their *gas-powered motor wagon*.

The *Granite Railway* was America's first commercial railroad.

Massachusetts was the first state to issue *license plates*.

America's first *subway* was built in Boston in 1867.

Little Brewster Island's *Boston Light* was the first lighthouse built in America.

Visitors tour Boston on a *duck boat* that can travel on land and water.

Rainbow Fleet is a colorful parade during Nantucket Race Week.

At the Boston University Bridge, a boat can sail under a train going under a vehicle driving under an airplane!

The Inland Waterway is home to a thrilling two-day *outboard race*.

Longer than three football fields, the *Paul R. Tregurtha* is the largest boat to pass through Sault Ste. Marie's *Soo Locks*.

Grand Rapids was famous for personalizing its streetcars. The *Spirit of St. Louis* streetcar was named in honor of the aviator Charles Lindberg.

There's an *80-foot-tall tire* in Allen Park.

Ford, Chrysler, General Motors, and Buick all started in Michigan.

Traverse City has one of the most popular pathways for *fat-tire biking*.

Carts once carried ore from Ironwood's *iron mines*.

Cars are banned on *Mackinac Island*.

The first *car assembly line* was invented in Highland Park in 1913.

MICHIGAN
The Great Lakes State

Built in Detroit in 1908, Henry Ford's *Model T* put the world on wheels.

It's illegal to drive with a **sheep in the car**—unless it has a chaperone.

Up to 500 cars can attend Butte's **Silver Bow Drive-In** movie theater.

Montana has more **hiking trails** than any other state.

Virginia City still looks like it did in the 1800s—complete with horse-pulled **stagecoaches**!

Missoula's **carousel** ponies were carved by volunteers.

The first **luge run** was built in Lolo Hot Springs.

Big Sky Resort is one of the **biggest ski resorts** in America.

MONTANA
The Treasure State

Red Lodge hosts an annual **motorcycle rally**.

Each of Glacier National Park's **Red Buses** are estimated to be worth $250,000.

Montana has three times more miles of **snowmobile trails** than interstate highways.

NEBRASKA
The Cornhusker State

A *cornhusker* is a person or machine that removes the husk from a corncob.

Carhenge is a Stonehenge replica made of cars.

Nebraska has a *lighthouse*, but it isn't anywhere near an ocean.

Floating in repurposed *stock tanks* is a fun way to enjoy Nebraska's rivers.

The first *chairlift* was invented in Nebraska.

On the *Bob Kerrey Pedestrian Bridge*, you can stand in both Nebraska and Iowa!

A giant *porch swing* in Hebron seats 17 people!

Nebraska's *Bailey Yard* is the largest railroad classification yard in the world.

New York City *subway cars* are built in Nebraska.

The world's largest collection of *historical roller skates* is in Lincoln.

NEW HAMPSHIRE
The Granite State

The **Lakes Region** has 273 lakes and ponds to kayak in.

The **Mount Washington Cog Railway** is the world's first mountain-climbing cog railway.

The oldest **motorcycle rally** in the world is held in Laconia.

The **Cornish-Windsor Bridge** is the longest wooden bridge in the United States.

There are more than 7,000 miles of **snowmobiling** trails in New Hampshire.

Born in Derry, astronaut **Alan Shepard** was the first American to travel into space.

Every car that reaches the 6,288 foot summit of **Mount Washington** receives a bumper sticker that says so.

Born in New Hampshire, inventor Thaddeus Lowe built a massive 103-foot **hot-air balloon**!

Over 750,000 vehicles drive the scenic **Kancamagus Highway** each year.

Lake Winnipesaukee has its own mail boat called the **Blue Ghost**.

The *high-flying tram* connecting Roosevelt Island and Manhattan can operate in winds up to fifty miles per hour.

In 1884, America's first *roller coaster* opened at *Coney Island*.

Traveling at supersonic speed, the *Concorde* once flew from New York to London in under three hours.

In April 1907, a record 197 ships carrying a quarter of a million passengers passed the *Statue of Liberty* on their way to Ellis Island.

The *NYC Subway* is made up of 25 routes.

The *Albany-Schenectady Railroad* was one of America's first railroads.

Boat passengers on *Maid of the Mist* in Niagara Falls receive complimentary rain ponchos.

Grand Central Terminal has 67 tracks, a tennis court, and a ceiling full of stars!

Twenty-one elephants once crossed over *Brooklyn Bridge* to demonstrate its strength.

Despite their iconic yellow color, the first *NYC cabs* were actually red and green!

NEW YORK
The Empire State

Charlotte Motor Speedway held the first official NASCAR Cup Series race.

Claremont's *Bunker Hill Covered Bridge* is over 125 years old.

America's *highest suspension footbridge* hangs from Grandfather Mountain's Linville Peak.

Jeep lovers gather at the *Jeeps on the Farm* festival in Denton.

Wilson is home to 30 *whirligigs*.

Blackbeard's *pirate ship* was discovered off the North Carolina coast in 1996.

Cape Hatteras is the tallest brick lighthouse in the United States.

The *Wright brothers* took off for the first time near Kitty Hawk.

Benson's *Mule Days* events include mule races and rodeos.

NORTH CAROLINA
The Tar Heel State

Cars aren't allowed on *Bald Head Island*.

NORTH DAKOTA
The Peace Garden State

North Dakota has the world's largest deposit of lignite, a type of soft, brown coal. It's been mined by *coal trucks* since 1873.

Red River cart trains were used to haul goods from Pembina.

The first time a *train* entered North Dakota was in 1872.

Theodore Roosevelt had *two ranches* in North Dakota.

Fargo Air Museum houses the *North American P-51D Mustang* from World War II.

Mountain hosts the *ND State Tractor & Pickup Pull*.

Skid-steer loaders were invented here in 1958.

The world's largest scrap metal sculptures sit along the *Enchanted Highway*.

Dunseith's *W'eel Turtle* is made of 2,000 tire rims.

In 1800s Medora, *stagecoach* rides cost 10 cents a mile.

OHIO
The Buckeye State

The first **police car** was used in Akron. It was electric.

In 1914, the nation's **first electric traffic light** was installed in Cleveland.

Tracy Pilurs's 1963 *DSA-1 miniplane* is on display at Ohio's International Women's Air & Space Museum.

There is a **tower of Volkswagen Beetles** in Defiance.

Every year, Elmore residents hold a **motorized casket race**.

Cleveland's **Cedar Point** has the most rides in one theme park.

Beavers can be spotted from the **Cuyahoga Valley Scenic Railroad**.

The **Toledo Jeeps** were a professional basketball team that played from 1946 to 1948.

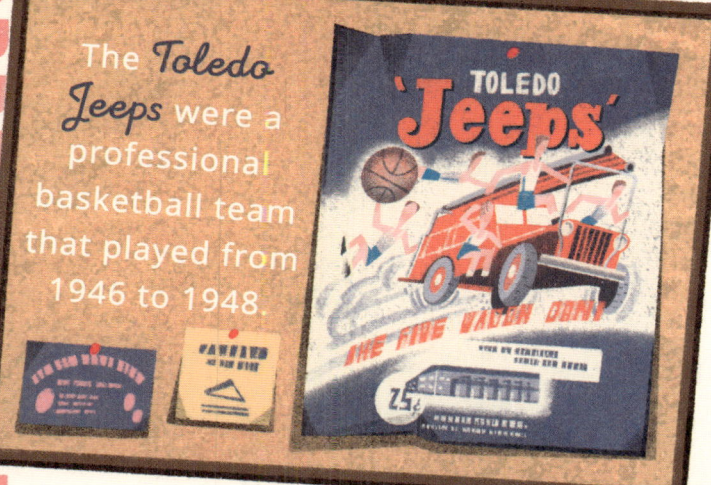

Cincinnati established the **first ambulance service** in the United States.

Akron is known as the "**rubber capital of the world.**"

TEXAS
The Lone Star State

Texas-born Wiley Post flew the **Lockheed Vega 5** to become the first pilot to fly solo around the world.

Rodeo is the state sport of Texas.

The **Johnson Space Center** is better known as "Mission Control" or "Houston."

At its peak, the **Rainbow Bridge** is the tallest bridge in Texas.

Texas State Highway 130 has the fastest speed limit in the country.

There is a collection of **10 Cadillacs** buried hood-first on a ranch near Amarillo.

Horses have long been an important mode of transport for the Comanche.

The **Texas Star** is the state's tallest Ferris wheel.

The **great Texas cattle drives** began in the 1860s to bring cattle to northern markets.

Hundreds of bats live under the **Congress Avenue bridge**.

UTAH
The Beehive State

The *Lagoon Roller Coaster* is more than 100 years old.

The *land speed record* at the Bonneville Salt Flats is 622 mph.

Boating is finally back on the Great Salt Lake after years of drought.

America's *first transcontinental railroad* was completed in Promontory in 1869. The rails were joined with a golden spike!

The last *SR-71 Blackbird* built is on display in Utah.

The 1.1-mile-long *Zion–Mount Carmel Tunnel* cuts through red sandstone.

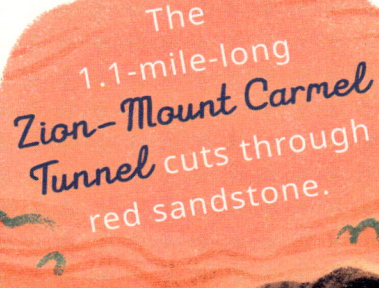

At Utah's Olympic Park, *the Comet Bobsled* reaches over 60 mph.

The *Mars Desert Research Station* prepares for human missions to Mars.

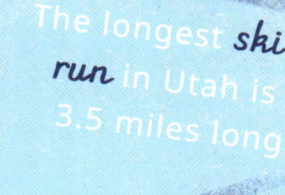

The longest *ski run* in Utah is 3.5 miles long.

The inventor of the *Zamboni* was born in Eureka.

WASHINGTON
The Evergreen State

Washington State Ferries is the biggest fleet in America. It carries more than 23 million people a year.

A version of *water skis* was invented in Bellevue.

Washington is home to the world's longest and widest *floating bridge*.

Washington apples are transported around the country on *semi-trucks*.

The Cascade Tunnel is the longest railroad tunnel in North America.

One of the first functional *flying cars*, the aero car, was built in Longview.

The first self-balancing *hoverboard* was invented in Camas.

Research vessels in Puget Sound monitor marine life.

The original *Seattle Center Monorail* trains from 1962 are still in use today.

The first *Lunar Rover* was built in Kent.

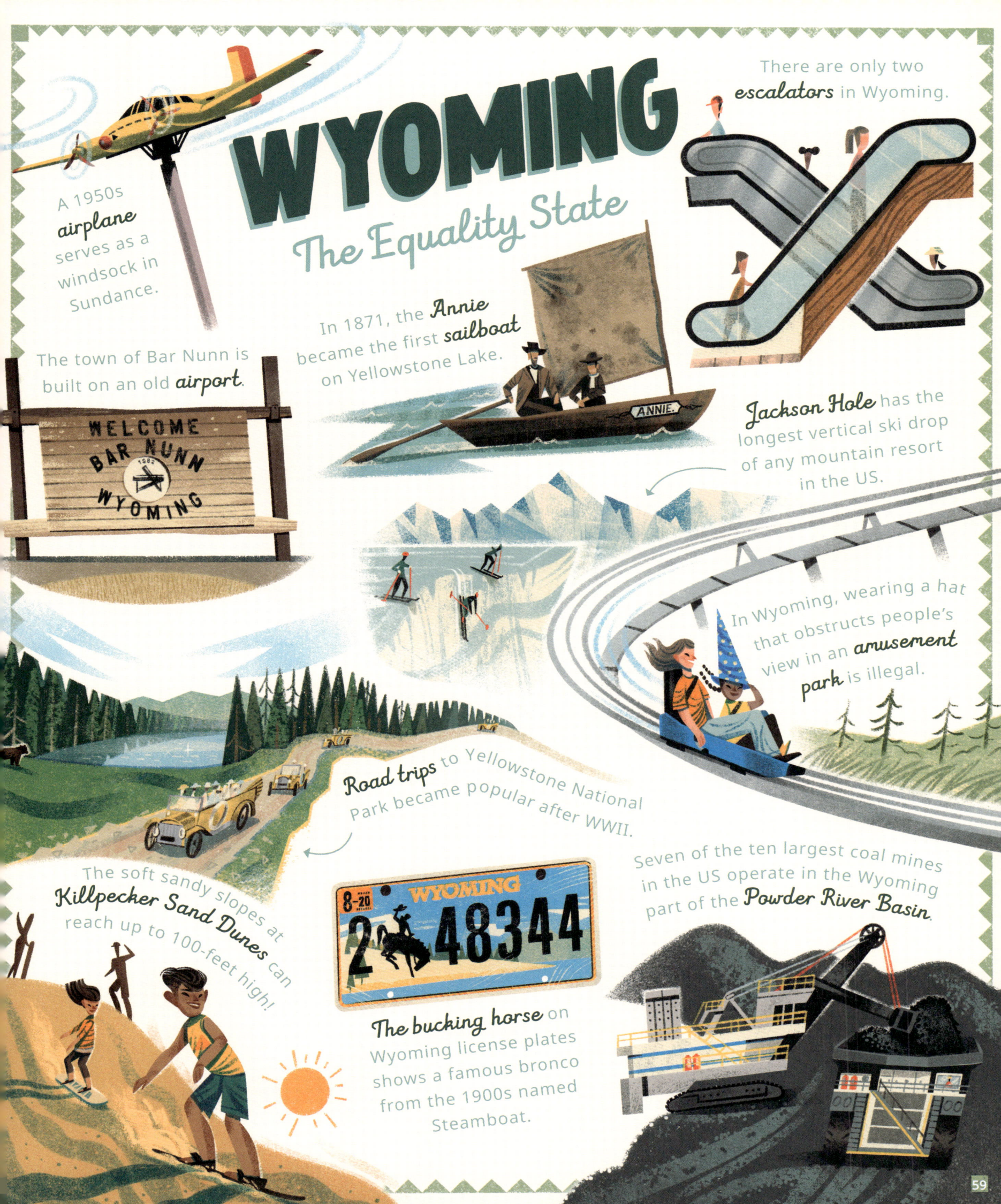

Index

A
air boat, 18
air show, 58
airplane, 15, 30, 41, 46, 55
    Boeing 727, 22
    Boeing KC-97, 15
    Concorde, 41
    DSA-1 miniplane, 44
    Lockheed Vega 5, 52
    P-51D Mustang, 43
    Spruce Goose, 46
    SR-71 Blackbird, 53
airport, 10, 19, 22, 33, 45, 59
airship, 19
Aldrin, Buzz, 10, 39
amusement park, 16
Anderson, Mary, 10
animal
    bald eagle, 57
    bat, 52
    beaver, 44
    dog, 11
    elephant, 41
    horse, 16, 26, 29, 34, 35, 47, 52
    mule, 12, 42
    mule deer, 21
    ostrich, 13
Appalachian Trail, 55
Armstrong, Neil, 10
ATV, 37, 57

B
baidarka, 11
Bancroft, Ann, 32
Barber, Gerald, 49
barge, 26, 51, 60
Baumgartner, Felix, 40
bicycle, 14, 31, 46, 49, 60
Blue Ridge Parkway, 55
boat, 26, 28, 29, 55
    Annie, The, 59
    Blue Ghost, 38
    Paul R. Tregurtha, 31
    Pilar, 18
    Stiletto, 48
    USS *Cairo*, 33
Bowen, Joe, 26
bridge, 42, 50
    Aerial Lift, 32
    Big Four, 26
    Bob Kerrey, 36
    Boston University, 30
    Brooklyn, 41
    Brush Creek, 25
    Chesapeake Bay, 55
    Congress Avenue, 52
    Cornish-Windsor, 38
    Eads, 34
    Fort Madison, 24
    Golden Gate, 14
    Lake Pontchartan Causeway, 27
    London, 12
    New River Gorge, 57
    Penobscot Narrows, 28
    Rainbow, 52
    Royal Gorge, 15
    Skydance, 45
    US-212 Missouri River, 50
bridge, covered, 54
    Bunker Hill, 42
    Stovall Mill, 19
bridge, floating, 56
    McDonald Memorial, 57
bridge, railroad
    Guffey, 21
    Carrollton Viaduct, 29
Bull, Toby Eagle, 50
bus, 24, 32, 35
byway, 21

C
cable car, 14
canoe, 20
car
    Buick, 31
    Cadillac, 33, 51, 52
    Chevrolet Corvette, 26
    Chrysler, 31
    Dawson Car, 55
    El Camino, 13
    Fawick Flyer, 50
    Ford Model T, 31
    Jeep, 42, 47
    Studebaker, 23, 60
carousel, 15, 23, 35, 48
chairlift, 36, 54
Chappelle, C. W., 19
Clinton, Bill, 13

D
drive-in, 19, 31, 34, 51
drive-through, 10, 12
Duryea, Frank and Charles, 30

E
Earhart, Amelia, 25
Endeavour, space shuttle, 14

F
Ferris wheel, 22, 45, 52
ferry, 16, 17, 56
festival, 10, 27, 40, 42, 46
floats, Mardi Gras, 10, 27
flying car, 56
flying saucer, 26, 49
food truck, 16, 49
Ford, Henry, 31
Froelich, John, 24
Fulton, Robert, 47

G
gondola (air), 21
gondola (boat), 23

H
helicopter, 12, 16, 20, 25
    VS-300, 16
Hemingway, Ernest, 18
highway, 11, 15, 18, 38, 47, 52
    Route 1, 28
    Route 23, 26
    Route 50, 37
    Route 66, 14, 25
    Route 100, 54
    Route 412, 45
hot-air balloon, 26, 34, 38, 40, 47
Hultgreen, Kara S., 16
Huyler Ramsey, Alice, 39

K
Kahanamoku, Duke, 20
kayak, 27, 37, 38
King, Martin Luther Jr., 60
Knievel, Evil, 21, 25

L
license plate, 17, 30, 55, 59
lighthouse, 19, 28, 30, 32, 33, 36, 39, 42, 48, 57

M
Marley, Bob, 17
metro, 60
miniature railroad, 34, 46
motorcycle, 16, 35, 38, 39
    Harley-Davidson, 50, 58
mountain bike, 13, 55
museum, 10, 12, 22, 23, 25, 43, 44, 49, 51, 60

O
off-roading, 12

P
Parkinson, John and Donald, 24
Parks, Rosa, 10
Parton, Dolly, 51
Pilur, Tracy, 44
pirates, 17, 42
Post, Wiley, 52
Presley, Elvis, 33
Purvis, William, 25

R
raceway, 39
racing
    bicycle, 17, 24
    boat, 19, 48
    car, 10, 14, 15, 18, 19, 23, 42, 49, 51, 55
    dragon boat, 19
    garden tiller, 13
    horse, 26, 29
    hot-air balloons, 34
    lawnmower, 23
    mattress, 32
    midget car, 45
    motorized casket, 44
    mules, 42
    outboard, 31
    outhouse, 11
    pumpkins, 46
    snowmobile, 28
    snowshoe, 32
    swamp buggy, 18
    toilet bowl, 50
    turkeys, 50
    wing suit, 12
railroad, 46, 51, 53
    Albany-Schenectady, 41
    Baltimore & Ohio, 29
    Black Hills Central, 50
    Florida East Coast, 18
    Granite, 30
    Mount Hood, 46
railroad, scenic
    Cuyahoga Valley, 44
    Fourth Street Elevator, 24
railway, cog
    Pikes Peak, 15
    Mount Washington, 38
Ride, Sally, 14
river
    Arkansas, 13
    Caddo, 13
    Chicago, 22
    Colorado, 12, 37
    Delaware, 39
    Green, 26
    Missouri, 50
    Potomac, 57
    Snake, 21
    St. Joe, 21
    Tennessee, 51
Rockefeller, John D. Jr., 28
rocket, 10, 14, 18, 21, 27, 33, 40, 52
rodeo, 15, 50, 52
roller coaster, 32, 41,
    Canyon Blaster, 37
    Excalibur, 28
    Kingda Ka, 39
    Lagoon, 53
    Smoky Mountain Alpine Coaster, 51
roller skating, 22, 27, 36
Roosevelt, Theodore, 43, 60
Rumsey, James, 57

S
sand dunes, 15, 59
satellite
    Explorer 1, 18
    Sputnik IV, 58
sculpture, 24, 32, 36, 37, 43, 44, 45, 49, 52, 55, 59
seaplane, 11
Shepard, Alan, 38
ship
    LST-325, 23
    MV *Columbia*, 11
    RMS *Queen Mary*, 14
    RMS *Titanic*, 50
    USS *Constellation*, 29
    USS *Yorktown*, 49
shipwreck, 17, 20, 54
skateboarding, 39, 50
skiing, 11, 21, 32, 35, 53, 54, 59
sky glider, 24
snowmobile, 11, 35, 38
steamboat, 33, 57
    American Queen, 27
    Clermont, The, 47
    Comet, The, 13
    Iowa, 24
    Savannah, The, 19
steam train, 15, 40, 57
Stevens, John, 39
storm chaser, 25, 45
street sign, 11, 45
streetcar, 13, 27, 31
submarine, 16
subway, 17, 30, 36, 41
surfing, 20, 58

T
tank, 19
theme park, 18, 21, 44
Thomas, Mamie, 33
train, 20, 22, 25, 43
    GG1, 47
    Potomac Eagle, 57
    Salt Mine Express, 25
tunnel
    Bobby Hopper, 13
    Cascade, 56
    Chesapeake Bay, 55
    Zion-Mount Carmel, 53
Tuskegee Airmen, 10

U
UFO, 28, 37, 40
underground railway, 23

W
Washington, George, 39
waterskiing, 32, 56
whitewater rafting, 28
Wilson, Charles, 25
Wright brothers, 42

Z
zamboni, 32, 53
zip wire, 57